THOUGHTS, PICTURES, AND WORDS

by

Karla Kuskin

photographs by

Nicholas Kuskin

 Richard C. Owen Publishers, Inc.
Katonah, New York

Meet the Author titles

Verna Aardema *A Bookworm Who Hatched*
David A. Adler *My Writing Day*
Frank Asch *One Man Show*
Joseph Bruchac *Seeing the Circle*
Eve Bunting *Once Upon a Time*
Lynne Cherry *Making a Difference in the World*
Lois Ehlert *Under My Nose*
Jean Fritz *Surprising Myself*
Paul Goble *Hau Kola Hello Friend*
Ruth Heller *Fine Lines*
Lee Bennett Hopkins *The Writing Bug*
James Howe *Playing with Words*
Johanna Hurwitz *A Dream Come True*

Karla Kuskin *Thoughts, Pictures, and Words*
Thomas Locker *The Man Who Paints Nature*
Jonathan London *Tell Me a Story*
George Ella Lyon *A Wordful Child*
Margaret Mahy *My Mysterious World*
Rafe Martin *A Storyteller's Story*
Patricia McKissack *Can You Imagine?*
Patricia Polacco *Firetalking*
Laurence Pringle *Nature! Wild and Wonderful*
Cynthia Rylant *Best Wishes*
Seymour Simon *From Paper Airplanes to Outer Space*
Jean Van Leeuwen *Growing Ideas*
Jane Yolen *A Letter from Phoenix Farm*

Text copyright © 1995 by Karla Kuskin
Photographs copyright © 1995 by Nicholas Kuskin

Richard C. Owen Publishers, Inc.
P.O. Box 585
Katonah, New York 10536

Library of Congress Cataloging-in-Publication Data

Kuskin , Karla .
  Thoughts, pictures, and words / by Karla Kuskin ; photographs by Nicholas Kuskin .
    p . cm . — (Meet the author)
    ISBN 1-878450-41-7
    1 . Kuskin , Karla — Biography — Juvenile literature . 2 . Authors, American— 20th century — Biography — Juvenile literature .
3 . Authorship — Juvenile literature . I . Kuskin , Nicholas.
II . Title . III . Series : Meet the author (Katonah , N . Y .)
PS3561 . U79Z474 1995
818 ' . 5409 — dc20
[B]   95-1290
                                                                CIP

Editor, Art, and Production Director *Janice Boland*
Editorial/Production Assistant *Peter Ackerman*
Color separation by Leo P. Callahan Inc., Binghamton, NY

Printed in the United States of America

9 8 7 6 5 4 3

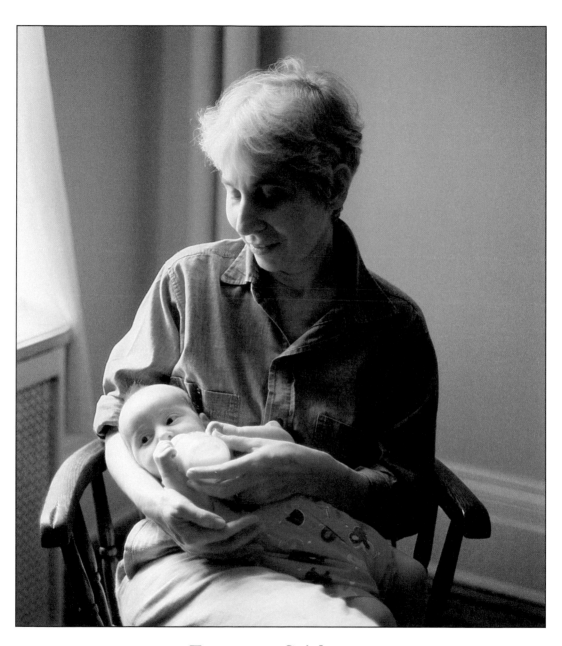

*For some Seidmans,
some Kuskins and Bells*

I go back and forth a lot.
In Brooklyn Heights
I live in an old red brick house.

And I work in a big upstairs room.

This is the view from our apartment across the river to Washington D.C.. You can see the Capitol, the Washington monument and the Lincoln Memorial.

In Arlington, Virginia, where my husband Bill Bell has an apartment overlooking Washington, D.C., I work at a desk in the bedroom.

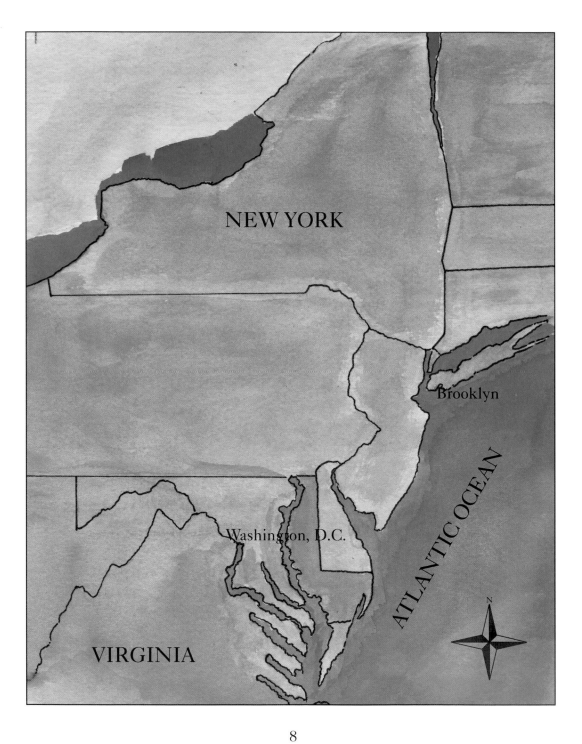

NEW YORK

Brooklyn

VIRGINIA

Washington, D.C.

ATLANTIC OCEAN

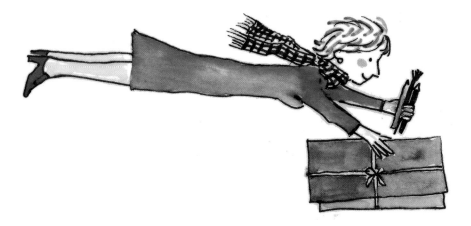

Me — flying back and forth.

Every couple of weeks I pack up
whatever I'm working on and fly
or take the train from one desk to the other.

I go back and forth in my work, too,
from poetry to prose,
and from writing to illustrating.

11

Sometimes I work on more than one project at a time.
When I wrote this book
I was also working on the pictures
for a book about a city dog
who goes back and forth to the country.
And I was putting my next collection
of poems together.

I don't really work
with a set schedule.
Instead, I do whatever
has to be done first.
I draw for a while,
then I put in the wash.
I get the mail,
then I make a phone call.

I think I write books because I loved reading them
so much as a child.
I loved drawing, too. Many of my feelings
and ideas come from my childhood.
I was born in Manhattan a long time ago.
The year I turned four we rented an old house
in Connecticut.

My room was spacious and had a very big closet.
I had lots of stuff, clothes and toys, that
I would leave lying all over the room.
My mother was not as happy about this as I was.
One day she got especially annoyed at my messiness
and told me to clean up the room immediately.
So I pushed, pulled, and carried until
I had gotten my desk and lamp,
my table and toys, my clothes, and chair,
everything but my bed, into my closet.
Then, triumphantly shutting the door on it all,
I called my mother.

My neat room in Connecticut

"See how neat my room is?" I said.
My mother thought that was funny,
and I remember how delighted I was
to have made her laugh.
I often put funny things into my books
because I'm still fond of jokes, of laughing,
and of making people laugh.

When I was in the third grade
we moved to Greenwich Village
in downtown Manhattan.
We lived right across the street
from the library.
Every week I took out
piles of books and after school
I would curl up with a book,
cookies, and milk.

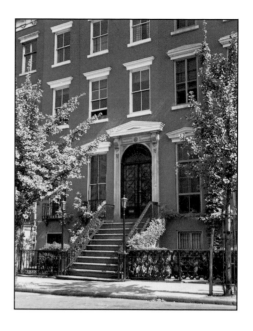

There was no television
in those days, and I
think that was lucky for
me. Without TV, or
brothers or sisters to
play with, I learned to
entertain myself. I got
used to daydreaming,
and writing and drawing.

In college I studied graphic design.
When everyone was given an assignment
to design and print a book,
I decided to make a picture book.
Our class had a small, motor-driven printing press,
and I used the different kinds of letters that we printed
with to show the different animal noises.

I called my book *Roar and More*
and it became my first published book.
After I got out of college,
I worked for a fashion photographer,
but I wasn't very good at that.
Then I worked on a magazine,
and then in an advertising agency,
writing copy and doing layouts.
I also wrote and illustrated another children's book
called *James and the Rain*.
I had married Charles Kuskin, an oboe player,
whose studio was at home.
I decided to stay at home too,
and work at my writing and illustrating full time.

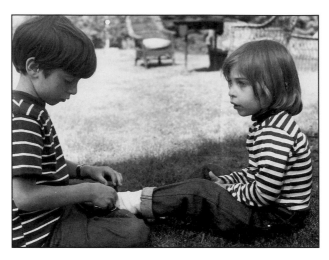

When our son Nicholas was born,
we moved to a house in Brooklyn.
A few years later our daughter Julia was born.
When she was in high school Charles and I divorced.
Now my children are grown up.

Julia works at graphic art.

Nick is a photographer
and took the pictures for this book.
His wife Mary is a pharmacist.
They are the parents of Madeleine Margaret,
my amazing granddaughter.

Several years ago I
married Bill Bell and
gained a new family:
Joel, Allison and
George, Bill and
Susan, and their
wonderful son Jake.

Despite all the changes in my life,
I'm still working in this room.
And it is even messier than my
Connecticut room was, because
I surround myself with things
I like to look at: old dolls, pictures
and frames, and rusty machinery.
Sometimes I think that the
inside of my head must resemble
my work room - a sort of attic full
of old thoughts, jokes, images,
rhymed and rhythmic lines-
the stuff that I use in my stories and poems.

The inside of my head

I have written a number
of books of poems.
I think I inherited my
versifying from my father.
He wrote verses to me on my
birthdays, on Valentine's Day,
and as letters when I was away
from home.

When I'm invited to speak
to classes of children and teachers,
one of the questions I'm most often asked is,
"Where do you get your ideas?"
I ask back, "When you write a story or poem
where do you get *your* ideas?"

Where do you get the idea for a poem?
Pippety
Poppety
Peep.
Does it shake you awake?
Do you dream it asleep?
Or into your tiny tin head does it creep
And pop from your pen when you are not aware
Or leap from your pocket
Or fall from your hair
Or is it just silently
Suddenly
There?...

I suspect the answer is that you, like me,
remembered something, saw something,
felt something that started you thinking.
It could be anything — a cat, for instance.

Toots' Nose

There is no nose I know
no nose I think
no point as pale and pink
a rose among fur snows.
If I could choose
to be a snoot as suitable
as it that sits on Toots
I would have chose
to be that very nose.

I got the idea for *The Philharmonic Gets Dressed*
when I saw how interested my children were
watching their father get dressed for a concert.
One idea can lead to another.
A reader in Israel, who liked
The Philharmonic Gets Dressed,
invited me to visit the city of Jerusalem.

I met many people and saw many places there,
and when I came home I spent a lot of time
thinking about what I had seen and learned.
Then I wrote *Jerusalem Shining Still*,
a short history of that city.
Making it short was hard because
the history of Jerusalem is long.
The city is 4,000 years old.

Any idea can be the beginning for a story.
Then all you need is the middle and an end...

> Without a beginning
> you wouldn't need an ending
> without a piece of paper
> you wouldn't need a pen
> consider the beginning
> then when you reach the ending
> go back to the beginning
> and begin again...
> again

I think that verse is about the way I work.
Trying to get a story or poem
just the way you want it is hard work.
I spend a great deal of time re-writing.
But I am very happy, working in my room at my desk,
in Brooklyn or Virginia, making pictures
and pushing words around.
So I just keep at it.

AUTHOR
Karla Kuskin

GEAUGA
COUNTY
YOUNG
AUTHORS'
CONFERENCE

WHEN DO WE LAUGH?

is where I came in

I CARE

Amigos de Mario Cuomo

Clinton Gore

BADGE MOUNT SE

INCOMING

CALIFORNIA
KARLA

Other Books by Karla Kuskin

Soap Soup and Other Verses; *Which Horse is William?*; *City Dog*; *Patchwork Island*; *Paul*; *City Noise*; *Dogs and Dragons, Trees and Dreams*; *The Dallas Titans Get Ready for Bed*.

About the Photographer

Nicholas Kuskin is a professional photographer and the son of Karla Kuskin. He grew up in the red brick house in Brooklyn, where most of the pictures for this book were taken. Nick lives in New York City with his wife Mary and their daughter Madeleine. He is restoring an old wooden boat which is docked on the Hudson River.

Julia Kuskin

Acknowledgments

Original watercolors on pages 7, 9, 16, and 22 by Karla Kuskin. Photographs on pages 7, 15, and 20 appear courtesy of Karla Kuskin. Photographs on pages 14, 17, and 23 by Mitzi S. Seidman. Illustration on page 27 copyright © 1982 by Marc Simont from *The Philharmonic Gets Dressed* by Karla Kuskin; reprinted by permission of Harper Collins *Publishers*. Illustration on page 28 copyright © 1987 by David Frampton from *Jerusalem Shining Still* by Karla Kuskin; reprinted by permission of Harper Collins *Publishers*. Illustration on page 24 copyright © 1975 by Karla Kuskin from *Near The Window Tree* by Karla Kuskin; reprinted by permission of Harper Collins *Publishers*. Illustrations on page 18 from *Roar and More* copyright © 1956, 1990 by Karla Kuskin; reprinted by permission of Harper Collins *Publishers*. Photograph on page 32 appears courtesy of Julia Kuskin. Photograph of Julia Kuskin on page 20 by Cat Gwynn copyright © 1993. Map illustration by Janice Boland.